The Sovereign Self:
Unplugging from the Matrix of Expectation

By

Carmid Vileramis

Copyright © 2025, Resonant Path Press, LLC

All rights reserved.

ISBN: 979-8-9999455-1-8

The Sovereign Self: Unplugging from the Matrix of Expectation

ISBN 979-8-9999455-1-8 (paperback)

ISBN 979-8-9999455-0-1 (hardcover)

ISBN 979-8-9999455-2-5 (ebook)

All rights reserved. No part of this publication may be reproduced, distributed, or transmitted in any form or by any means, including photocopying, recording, or other electronic or mechanical methods, without the prior written permission of the publisher, except in the case of brief quotations embodied in critical reviews and certain other noncommercial uses permitted by copyright law.

Copyright © 2025, Resonant Path Press, LLC.

The information in this book is provided for educational purposes only and is not intended as professional advice. The author and publisher disclaim any liability for any adverse effects resulting from the use or application of the information contained herein.

This book is not intended as a substitute for professional medical or mental health advice, diagnosis, or treatment. Always seek the advice of qualified health providers, including physicians, therapists, psychiatrists, or psychologists, with any questions you may have regarding a medical or mental health condition. Never disregard professional medical advice or delay seeking it because of something you have read in this book. If you are experiencing a mental health emergency or having thoughts of self-harm, please contact your local emergency services, call 988 (Suicide & Crisis Lifeline), or contact a mental health crisis hotline immediately.

The author is not liable for any damages or negative consequences from any treatment, action, application, or preparation to any person reading or following the information in this book.

Individual results may vary, and this book does not guarantee specific outcomes.

While every effort has been made to ensure accuracy, the author and publisher assume no responsibility for errors, omissions, or damages arising from the use of this information.

The views expressed in this book are those of the author and do not necessarily reflect the views of the publisher.

The Sovereign Self: Unplugging from the Matrix of Expectation

The Sovereign Self: Unplugging from the Matrix of Expectation

DEDICATION

To Thy Self.

The Sovereign Self: Unplugging from the Matrix of Expectation

CONTENTS

DEDICATION	iv
CONTENTS	v
ACKNOWLEDGMENTS	vii
FOREWORD	viii
PART 1 - REMEMBERING WHO YOU ARE	1
1. Who We've Been	1
2. The Veil of the World	7
PART 2 - UNPLUGGING FROM THE MATRIX	17
3. Deconstructing Identity	17
4. Honoring the Shadow	24
5. Your Inner Compass	30
PART 3 - LIVING AS THE INFINITE SELF	35
6. The Practice of Presence	35
7. Purpose As Frequency	39
8. Global Soul, Local Heart	42
PART 4 - THE COLLECTIVE AWAKENING	48
9. Dismantling the Old, Seeding the New	48
10. Infinite You	53
AI DISCLOSURE STATEMENT	i
GLOSSARY	iii
FURTHER READING	vi
ABOUT THE AUTHOR	ix

The Sovereign Self: Unplugging from the Matrix of Expectation

The Sovereign Self: Unplugging from the Matrix of Expectation

ACKNOWLEDGMENTS

I am thankful that my journey continues to evolve because of my light, shadows, and support network: family, friends, and therapist, all the souls I encounter on this ride. Grace.

The Sovereign Self: Unplugging from the Matrix of Expectation

FOREWORD

This journey began, as many profound transformations do, in the quiet depths of the night. It started as a simple journal entry on the first full day of the Spring Equinox, March 20, 2024—a time historically associated with renewal, balance, and new beginnings. Yet, what began as a personal reflection was swiftly "thwarted by a superpower," the universal consciousness I call "The All that Is".

My deepest desire in writing *The Sovereign Self: Unplugging from the Matrix of Expectation* is to meet you, the reader, at a crossroads. Perhaps you sense a stirring within, a yearning for something more authentic than what the external world offers, much like I once did, having lived a life steeped in the cultural dogma that dictates our worth and belonging--only to find it unfulfilling.

This book invites you to gather knowledge and empower yourself to continue your unique journey towards remembering the boundless truth of who you are, your inherent worth, and the power you hold to live authentically.

For over half a century, I have navigated this three-dimensional existence. I've learned that our true journey involves facing what we often dismiss or reject—our shadows, fears, and the illusions that keep us disconnected from our divine essence. This path is not always comfortable; it can bring forth inner conflicts. Yet, within this discomfort lies the profound opportunity for growth, transformation, and awakening.

The Sovereign Self: Unplugging from the Matrix of Expectation is a testament to the belief that you are the Source and ALL that Is.

The Sovereign Self is the part of you that existed before fear, conditioning, or identity. It's the original 'you' that no system can own.

You possess the innate ability to choose how you perceive experiences, to form and transform your belief system, and to create your world unapologetically. It is a philosophy not confined to any particular religion or spiritual guru, but inherently accessible to all. It's

The Sovereign Self: Unplugging from the Matrix of Expectation

reclaiming your birthright to inner freedom. It's a life aligned with your Higher Self—your unwavering North Star.

Throughout these pages, we will explore how to deconstruct inherited identities, honor the unseen parts of ourselves, trust our inner guidance, cultivate presence in a demanding world, and align our purpose with a higher frequency. We will discuss how personal transformation is inextricably linked to a global collective awakening, where old, divisive systems can give way to new ones rooted in compassion and respect.

I offer these observations and experiences with thoughtfulness and deep gratitude, hoping they catalyze your magnificent unfolding.

May this book be a collaborative whisper from the universe, reminding you of your infinite potential, your inherent worth, and the power you hold to create, transform, and live authentically.

I publish under this pseudonym to protect my privacy and allow me the freedom of expression without reservation or filters.

— Carmid Vileramis

The Sovereign Self: Unplugging from the Matrix of Expectation

The Sovereign Self: Unplugging from the Matrix of Expectation

PART 1 - REMEMBERING WHO YOU ARE

1. Who We've Been

Our true journey begins at night, when shadows and fears reveal what lies beneath the surface. That night in the forest, I encountered a shapeshifter—an embodiment of the unseen parts of myself—reminding me that the path to remembrance involves facing what we often dismiss or reject.

20 March 2024 - The first full day of the Spring Equinox. The intent of this journey began as a normal journal entry, then thwarted by a superpower, The All that Is, or the universal consciousness that is all-knowing, omnipresent, and connected to us all sentient beings. That Source ignited the fire within me to create this resource.

I was compelled to share my journey with those seeking a deeper understanding. It's a desire to meet readers at a crossroads where they can gather knowledge and empower themselves to enhance their journeys in a shifting world.

This was not my first journal entry. Journaling significant and mundane life events has been a continuous practice.

Turning my experiences into a book had been a passing thought that lay dormant inside me for several years, until that day, when inspiration called me to take action. It was a compulsion that filled me with excitement and anxiety, but I knew then, there would be no further delays.

The Sovereign Self: Unplugging from the Matrix of Expectation

It was fitting that this journey began on the Spring Equinox, a time of renewal, balance, and new beginnings.

The first crack in the Matrix started at a young age for me.

I was about 4 or 6 years old. Moving cautiously through the dense forest at night, my heart beat furiously. The air was thick, and all I could make out were the shapes of the trees towering over me, beneath the moon-filled sky.

I felt his eyes following my every step. I felt lost. I wanted to scream for my parents, but I quickly realized that, in this existence, I am all there is.

Something reaches down from above and taps my shoulder, startling me. I look up at a nearby tree, and there's a being who's part man and part panther. It's a shapeshifter. He stares at me and says nothing. Terrified, I wished him gone, only to feel remorse for my fear-based reaction later.

That was the only time I saw him. That is my earliest memory of other sentient beings outside the "waking world" who support me. In other words, I knew I was never alone.

It was as if I felt his hurt at my rejection. I was disappointed and thought I had let him down. Maybe we could've had more adventures together. Later, I realized the sadness came from me. Because we were connected spiritually, he felt what I was feeling.

Shapeshifting spirits or figures in folklore and mythology play various roles across different cultures, often embodying themes of transformation, adaptability, duality, and mystery.

My encounter was not malicious. He was a friend and protector who was there to comfort and initiate me into the invisible world. He made me aware that my waking state is not all there was. There is also the unseen world, where we commune with invisible beings of all varieties. It's where we lead with intuition and feelings, where dialogue isn't always needed to receive experiences. It's where we see entities, visions we don't normally see, and can do things we can't do in our waking state.

The Sovereign Self: Unplugging from the Matrix of Expectation

My childhood shapeshifter friend never spoke any words, but he made me aware he was only one of countless possible beings, giving me my first glimpse of the layered reality beyond the veil. I cannot say for certain that I would have ever questioned my world, as I have, if he had never made his presence known to me. I am grateful for that.

His shocking appearance laid the groundwork for my tolerance and acceptance of the unknown, even if logic couldn't explain away certain mysteries that don't adhere to convention.

The Sovereign Self: Unplugging from the Matrix of Expectation

The Sovereign Self: Unplugging from the Matrix of Expectation

Having lived in this 3-dimensional existence for over half a century, I understood it was time to commit to authoring my life as a true co-creator instead of a recipient of the external.

Carrying the emotional weight of cultural projections, which may or may not align with my values, for decades, takes its toll. I employed a careful vetting process when I purchased my first car, and when I decided on a suitable house or city to move to. Why not apply that attention to everything else I manifest in my life?

It is not, nor has it ever been, necessary to stay plugged into a culture that relies upon the affirmation of external sources to qualify my worthiness and sense of belonging.

Pursuing my passion and living my values throughout the last half of my journey is my purpose.

Gratitude, growth, selfless love, and a healthy sense of Self best honor my life and service to my community. If I do my very best to do that, in all its authenticity, I will have lived a life that I can call honorable.

Mindful of the gratitude that swims in my subconsciousness, it's important that I acknowledge both my accomplishments and failures.

While it pains me to have gone through certain experiences (some external and some by my own hands) I embrace those moments, not as a victim, but as a student and an avid learner poised to transform my challenges into memorable growth opportunities to transform me into better versions of myself—all in the service of my authentic Self. It's a Self that does not focus on regret but embraces all the parts of me that choose to receive challenges as tools for making myself better to thrive.

I am The Source. I am ALL that Is. I get to choose how I perceive experiences. Am I the victim or creator of my experiences? Will I dim my light to make others in my environment more comfortable, or do I value myself enough to unplug from that dogma

The Sovereign Self: Unplugging from the Matrix of Expectation

and pursue my passions unapologetically in ways that honor my Higher Self—my unconditioned truth?

I constantly question myself, guided by my heart—my North Star—to uphold the integrity of my values when faced with emotional discomfort and internal resistance. Even if I cannot pinpoint the source of my resistance, I recognize the feeling, which is enough for me to critically examine it and realign myself with Source.

My heart is the key to staying on course and pursuing my passion and purpose. It is instrumental in navigating the narrative I manifest, not my brain. The brain delays manifestation with fear-based logic.

Trying to navigate the "how" of my manifestations is an exercise in futility. It is enough to know that I know my desires are realized. I am in charge of creating my world. Recognizing the external forces that labor to control my autonomy is a sobering journey.

Humanity's shared trait is that we are divinely connected. Remembering our shared divine connection is a powerful navigational tool containing a rich and unique blueprint for each of us, one that is too important to forget or not put down our temporary societal masks to explore.

As we journey through life, we often carry the weight of expectations—those of family, society, and our tendency to judge ourselves harshly. In this chapter, I invite you to reflect on your formative experiences.

Consider the messages you received about who you should be. Were they rooted in love, fear, or something else entirely? By acknowledging these influences, we can begin dismantling the narratives that no longer serve us.

Reflection Prompt: Reflect on a moment when fear or illusion obscured your understanding of your true self. How did you move through it? What did it teach you? Write down three key moments from your past that shaped your identity. How do they resonate with who you are today?

The Sovereign Self: Unplugging from the Matrix of Expectation

2. The Veil of the World

Most people live their entire lives inside a story they didn't write. Before we're conscious enough to question it, it's laid out for us by parents and institutions. It's fed to us as truth, while it's anything but.

The Sovereign Self begins to awaken the moment you notice the story. The awakening starts as a harmless curiosity that morphs into a gradual shift, the moment the veil begins to lift. Once you get a glimpse, you can never unsee it.

The world's chaos often masks the deeper truth of our collective awakening. Witnessing division, injustice, and upheaval signals a profound opportunity—an invitation to look inward and question the illusions that keep us disconnected from our divine essence.

An election happened, in which a nation elected an archaic symbol of gluttony, corruption, crime, and hate to represent it, for a second time.

The level of societal discord, disinformation, tribalism, and public service dysfunction impacting the lives of the average working-class people is one that I have not witnessed in my lifetime. It's significant because it can disrupt one's sense of security, leaving us dissatisfied.

The Sovereign Self: Unplugging from the Matrix of Expectation

In this example, an election result is not the sole cause of the discord, but a consequence stemming from decades of supportive institutions and antithetical shared norms, which cannot be oversimplified by pointing to a political persuasion.

Our soul tells us to seek resolution and harmony to mitigate the tension.

While some may disagree, I see this as a unique opportunity. One that offers people a chance to dismantle an existing power structure whose institutions are built from an inherently racist, divisive, and colonialist mindset, leaving little room for co-existence based on compassion and respect.

Following the history of a modern capitalist society, socio-economic structures like the US are fueled by discord.

It fosters a cultural narrative in which only a few in the wealthiest class perpetually hold power.

Such cultural trends lend themselves to the injustices of religious crusades, wars, genocides, slavery, theft of indigenous lands, the purging of indigenous peoples, and the very constitution that shaped the American government. The divide-and-conquer approach that pits communities against each other epitomizes governing bodies with authoritarian incentives.

The narrative of oppressive dominance over the masses has proven historically profitable for the wealthiest few. It follows the well-documented history of slave labor, which played a crucial role in the capitalist structure.

C.L.R. James's *The Black Jacobins* gives a historical account of how a developing European capitalism, and later in the Americas, is fundamentally linked to the barbaric system of slave labor on plantations in Saint-Domingue, Hispaniola (modern-day Haiti), leading up to the Haitian Revolution, ending French colonial rule and slavery.

In this pivotal moment of our history, the ruling classes behind corporate interests appear to be landing monumental victories over the working classes, to the point where many are convinced that fortifying borders and prioritizing nationalism over humanitarianism is sustainable. If a ruling class, while concentrating its power, can

The Sovereign Self: Unplugging from the Matrix of Expectation

successfully gaslight populations into abandoning their critical thinking skills and desire for introspection, it will lead them to desperation and defeat.

A defeated collective consciousness can take the form of brutality and a complete breakdown of the system, compelling one to face oneself, retreat inward, and question the belief systems with which they once identified.

It can be disconcerting to watch world events depict images of civil unrest. Then, some moments can grip you emotionally, causing you to shift your emotional passivity to a relatability that profoundly impacts you.

In my case, seeing the rising tensions against immigrant communities and the manufactured narratives developed to demonize people escaping hardships from their native countries, only to be met with violence and family separations, was especially hurtful. As a child of immigrant parents (I was born in New York State) who sought a better life for me and my siblings, I was particularly moved by the cruelty, hurt, and lack of empathy surrounding these communities.

My parents were extremely proud when they became naturalized U.S. citizens in 1975. I remember family trips to Washington, D.C., visiting historical monuments and museums. Those were fun times. My parents found time to relax, bond with their children, and visit friends.

Decades later (2018), I received a call from my mother, then a retiree (my dad had already passed away), who was in tears. Her voice was shaky from both anger and hurt. She had seen a widely circulated news soundbite of her country's president, referring to her native country, among some others, as "shithole countries." It shocked many nations worldwide to hear a president use such vulgar language, but especially my mother. Naturally, it hurt me to hear how she was hurting.

It was one of the more impactful moments of awareness that compelled me to look deeper at who I am and review my sense of belonging and community.

Self-reflection and the deconstruction of one's ego do not traditionally come easily for many humans. People who consciously or subconsciously internalize the identity of their culture and its social norms are likely to experience challenges with defining their authentic selves and opening up to the personal journeys it entails. Those journeys divert from group

The Sovereign Self: Unplugging from the Matrix of Expectation

thinking and internal conflict that may lead to a "dark night of the soul" moment, where one encounters a transformative phase in their life in which internal conflicts surface for them, which comes from the writing of St. John of the Cross, a 16th-century Spanish Carmelite monk and mystic who described a period of spiritual purification and transformation in a poem of the same title.

When facing this moment, one is pushed to take stock of their value system, release those that no longer serve them, and embrace values that foster growth.

Another example where such inner conflicts may present themselves is when a society that perpetuates the corrosive patterns of socio-economic inequity and institutional racism, placing personal and environmental well-being in the hands of leaders who commodify war, division, the privatization of public services, and deference to corporate interests over the working class.

As people sense dysfunction and a breakdown in the judicial system, civil unrest and rising class tensions follow, amplified by mainstream media outlets and religious institutions aligning themselves with cultural conventions that assume the conformity of their citizens.

As a result, the grumblings of dissent lead to a cultural awakening and soul searching driven by love and bodily autonomy. It threatens to upend the one in place and fundamentally opposes the fruition of a society that questions its ruling class and insists on oversight.

We've reached a critical moment in the history of our ever-shifting world. The combination of institutional racism that permeates the capitalist and authoritarian systems we've come to recognize in certain countries has fused in a way that exposes pseudodemocracies for what they truly are—performative gestures failing to meet society's needs.

These failures remain largely unvalidated as a general societal condition. Misguided cultural narratives and propaganda distract the masses. Super-billionaires can buy their way

The Sovereign Self: Unplugging from the Matrix of Expectation

to the ears of influential politicians and community leaders who are fully invested in their special interests.

Societies are increasingly cognizant of the collateral damage inflicted by disinformation, which has landed them in compromising situations. They have witnessed the abject insensitivity and betrayal of their elected officials, who continue to deprive them of essential public services.

How can a new and improved consciousness sprout if we hang on to the decaying corpse of an antiquated one that is self-serving and divisive? It cannot. It must first die.

The old must die to make way for a sustainable culture that thrives by facing its shadows, finds strengths in its discovery, and continuously strives to improve.

A vision of a thriving culture is tenable and consists of a collective consciousness in which its people willfully embark on an immersive journey to identify with its authentic self.

It's a Self that is altruistic, compassionate, and in harmony with values in service of a greater good.

The mouse that is content scavenging for crumbs that have fallen off the buffet table will never realize it's at a banquet until it looks up.

The world often presents a façade—a veil obscuring the truth of our shared humanity. We are taught to see differences instead of recognizing the common threads that connect us all. This chapter challenges you to look beyond the surface. What lies beneath the labels of race, gender, and class?

Every seeker sees the disconnect between what they've been taught and what they feel is true. This noticing is the start of sovereignty.

Collective awakening involves lifting the veil on illusions we mistake for truth.

This can involve a variety of tools that one may find useful for deconstructing illusions.

The Sovereign Self: Unplugging from the Matrix of Expectation

As the intended audience for this book is the general reader, the following suggested tools are accessible whether you are a spiritual seeker, social activist, or hold a general interest in this subject matter.

1. Meditation and mindful practices

    a. Collective mindfulness: Group meditation practices can create a shared energy field and promote unity and compassion, according to Number Analytics [*Lee, S. (n.d.). The power of collective mindfulness. https://www.numberanalytics.com/blog/the-power-of-collective-mindfulness*]. *This enhances your sensitivity to others in your community and the plight of your neighbors. It inspires empathy, compassion, and activism.*

    b. Mindful movement and breath-work exercises: Yoga practices, or conscious breathing, when done in a group, can deepen individual and collective awareness.

2. Promoting critical thinking and open dialogue

    a. Encourage open dialogue in safe, inclusive spaces where people can share differing views respectfully. Debate is critical for challenging collective illusions. This can be promoted within communities and organizations. I am compelled to emphasize the importance of in-person gatherings vs online meetings. While there are advantages to online engagement, like accommodating individuals with limited mobility and a broader outreach, if in-person meetings can be facilitated, they should be encouraged. In-person engagements can meet the social needs of individuals receptive to physical presence in their community. *These activities can open up opportunities for diverse groups of varying opinions and values to exchange ideas that foster supportive environments. The momentum can incentivize and grow community ties.*

    b. Seeking evidence and challenging assumptions: Instead of passively accepting information, individuals and groups can actively and respectfully question the basis of beliefs and decisions, asking for data evidence to support them. Acquiring supportive evidence on community topics (e.g., opposition to banning books at their local library) by collecting signatures, testimonials, or surveys from community members is a validating action that can lead to activism, unexpected local public officers, and effective policy change.

The Sovereign Self: Unplugging from the Matrix of Expectation

  c. Practicing self-awareness: Regularly reflecting on one's beliefs and comparing them to perceived group norms can help address potential blind spots or biases. Asking yourself or journaling your thoughts on why you might oppose same-sex relationships can prompt you to examine your preconceived notions. New questions may arise regarding why limiting compassion and equity to certain groups is or isn't justified.

3. Education and critical pedagogy

  a. Learner-centered approaches: Critical pedagogy emphasizes that learners are active participants in their education, and learning should involve problem-solving, theoretical, and practical understanding. Research climate change—compare local sources with global ones. Consider using gamification techniques to bring communities together while integrating learning. There are useful gamification tools like Kahoot!, in which anyone with a cell phone can participate in learning events, take fun quizzes, and polls, which facilitate systemic restructuring of how learners receive and disseminate information.

  b. Challenging dominant narrative: Critical pedagogy encourages educators to make biases and power structures visible, inviting learners to question the norms and decisions that shape institutions and society. Analyze how you can discern how climate change is represented in various communities and media outlets. Is there a bias in how different local publications represent climate change? Are lawmakers on the same page as their constituents on the topic?

  c. Fostering intellectual humility: Encouraging a willingness to revise opinions based on new evidence and creating spaces for dissent helps to counter irrational thinking and groupthink. Does all the evidence you found on climate change disrupt or reinforce your existing convictions? Consider how you might deliver your findings at your community centers. Think of ways to engage in diverse discussions that foster non-judgment and are conducive to speaking openly and respectfully.

4. Art and creative expression for social commentary

The Sovereign Self: Unplugging from the Matrix of Expectation

    a. Reflecting and shaping societal values: Artists can use their work to mirror and critique societal norms, values, and institutions, promoting critical thinking and fostering awareness about important issues like inequality and injustice.

    b. Using satire, symbolism, and imagery, Artists can employ various techniques to convey complex messages and spark dialogue about social issues. *For example, Frida Kahlo explored themes of identity and feminism through her self-portraits, calling attention to themes of inequity.*

    c. Leveraging the digital age: Social media and other platforms have expanded to reach and impact of art as a form of social commentary, allowing artists to raise awareness and mobilize support for social causes. Be mindful that social media has limitations with its reach. Technology gaps exist in some communities. *Social media and AI technologies can be used to showcase the plight of the homeless and the lack of healthcare in rural and underserved communities.*

5. Engaging in philosophy and dialectical reasoning

    a. Socratic method: This involves questioning assumptions, clarifying ideas, identifying contradictions, and guiding individuals toward a clearer, more consistent understanding, while encouraging intellectual humility and self-reflection.

    b. Dialectical reasoning: Involves analyzing arguments by challenging one's view with its opposite, aiming to find truth and understanding in the interplay of these opposing perspectives. Employ this method to gauge popular assumptions about progress. Investigate and open a respectful dialogue on progress as defined by Western culture. Ask questions like, "Is endless progress a good idea?" Compare those assumptions to those of other cultures and reflect on how dissenting views might deconstruct the norm.

6. Indigenous wisdom and knowledge systems

    a. Decolonization of knowledge: Centering Indigenous epistemologies challenges dominant Western knowledge systems and promotes a more nuanced understanding of the world, fostering decolonization and social justice. Learning about how Indigenous communities view their two-spirited community members with reverence may

The Sovereign Self: Unplugging from the Matrix of Expectation

give other communities some perspective and insight into the many ways in which LGBTQ community members are valued and have a role in the universal consciousness, as every other human does.

    b. Reconnecting with the land and community: Indigenous education emphasizes a curriculum consciousness of the land, language, and community, fostering a deep understanding of the environment and a sense of belonging. *Adding Indigenous perspectives on our connection to the land can reshape how other cultures view their relationship to the earth and each other, mitigating their impact on climate change.*

7. Social activism and community organizing

    a. Collective action and advocacy: Community organizing mobilizes individuals to address systemic injustices and promote social justice through collective action and advocacy for policy changes

    b. Building coalitions and partnerships: Working with other organizations and communities can strengthen collective power and drive social change, especially with marginalized communities. Both kinds of advocacy are impactful because organized communities that gather peacefully can be impactful, as safety tends to be in large numbers (in most cases). Silent activism can be just as impactful. Boycotting large organizations by refusing to purchase their products.

Withholding your consumer dollars and getting others in your community to do the same is a powerful tool for deconstruction.

8. Journaling and self-reflection

    a. Enhanced self-awareness and emotional processing: Journaling offers a safe space to explore thoughts and feelings, identify patterns, process emotions, and improve mental clarity. *Parsing out your core values vs inherited ones can inspire creativity and enthusiasm for wanting to motivate others to liberate their paradigms with thoughtful exploration.*

    b. Challenging negative beliefs: Journaling can help individuals identify and reframe negative thoughts, fostering a more positive and realistic perspective, *according to Duke Health and Well-being [De Montjoye, C. (2023, October 18). The Power of Journaling for Well-*

The Sovereign Self: Unplugging from the Matrix of Expectation

being: A Path to Self-Discovery and Healing - DHW blog. DHW Blog. https://dhwblog.dukehealth.org/the-power-of-journaling-for-well-being-a-path-to-self-discovery-and-healing/]

At work, my team explores educational technology delivery methods to enhance higher education curriculum. When researching applications, I remain mindful of technological gaps within certain communities, accessibility considerations for web users with disabilities, and the potential biases in assessment questions. By challenging the dominant narrative around curriculum design, I help cultivate a space where standardized narratives are challenged and enhanced active learning is accessible to diverse adult learners.

Consider this: When we peel back these layers, we find a shared desire for connection, understanding, and love. Let us begin to lift the veil together, acknowledging our shared humanity.

Reflection Prompt: Identify one societal or personal belief that keeps you separate or disconnected. How might recognizing this illusion bring you closer to your true self?

The Sovereign Self: Unplugging from the Matrix of Expectation

PART 2 - UNPLUGGING FROM THE MATRIX

3. Deconstructing Identity

I was 20 years old and having a vivid dream where a beautiful, young, white lady with dark curly hair and hazel eyes motioned to me to follow her into a fancy Victorian home with many rooms.

She appeared as an aristocrat dressed in an 18th-century formal party dress and satin/lace gloves. She extended her hand for me to grab hold so I could follow her through the courtyard and into this mansion. She said she had something to show me, and it was a secret.

I was then led through the foyer and up a marble staircase toward the very top level of the home. We soon found ourselves out on the rooftop. She then turned to me and whispered, "Don't tell anybody this, but my mother was black." She then tightened her grip on my hand and began flying, with me alongside her. Soon, we were soaring amongst the clouds over what appeared to be a modern European city. I was transfixed and elated at the feeling of freedom and secrecy of our adventure. Flying felt like my soul's ultimate expression of freedom, where anything was possible.

In the dream, I felt a sense of awe in her presence. She was a woman of great sophistication and wealth, yet she made me feel like we were equals by sharing her secret, which made her much more relatable. I didn't feel out of place with her as my companion.

The Sovereign Self: Unplugging from the Matrix of Expectation

Based on the woman's description and how she made me feel, I believe that she was Erzulie Freda, a powerful and complex spirit (or loa) of Haitian Vodou tradition.

She is associated with love, beauty, and femininity, often depicted as a beautiful light-skinned (mulatto) woman. She is also associated with jealousy, heartache, and the complexities of human relationships.

That was the year I experienced my first travel abroad for a year in the UK during my junior year in college as part of an international exchange program. I have had a profound love for traveling and experiencing other cultures since.

That prophetic dream awakened my heart and consciousness, awakening me to an expansive exploration of my identity, beliefs, and all the forces that lead me to question the worldview. Freda helped me to understand that my identity transmutes between my soul and body. Her appearing to me in that particular setting also spoke to the mindset of enslavement and activating my ability to liberate myself from the societal trappings that enslave me with limiting beliefs, which may keep me from realizing my potential.

My soul is not confined to the third-dimensional body that I currently inhabit, which adheres to the laws of the land. It bifurcates to a version of myself that is an all-knowing observer, and my body is the "experiencer" of the content being observed. My essence is the sovereign All that Is and the seed of my inner freedom.

The Sovereign Self: Unplugging from the Matrix of Expectation

The Sovereign Self: Unplugging from the Matrix of Expectation

This philosophy isn't one of any particular religion or spiritual guru. It is accessible to all. No subscription or initiation is required to adopt it, for tapping into your inner freedom is an inherent right.

Living harmoniously with our fellow man and planet is the legacy of early humans that can be reclaimed. As cultural shifts, modernity and power structures took shape, our universal unity transformed into individualism and ego-driven marginalization facilitated by fear-based cultural influences, like media saturation, technology, religion, and wars.

Deconstructing one's identity is key to learning to tap into the authentic self. It's the core "you"-the Higher Self- ever-present in all your life experiences.

Part of what shapes our identity and consciousness is the societal structures in which we live.

The concept of "The Matrix," as portrayed in the popular film of the same name, may come to mind.

"The Matrix film (1999)" depicts a simulated reality where humans are unknowingly plugged (literally) into a system that controls their thoughts, beliefs, and actions. This can be seen as a metaphor for societal structures and cultural norms, which can significantly influence individual identities.

In this book, I explicitly use the Matrix to reference a metaphor for societal systems influencing individual belief systems, not the movie; unplugging is the *psychological* act of discerning the authentic from the constructed.

I once worked as an administrative assistant for an attorney with questionable work ethics.

Part of my role was to process department payments for various vendor services and teaching faculty. I noticed a payment he authorized for a particular faculty, who was also one of his mentors. He cleared that

The Sovereign Self: Unplugging from the Matrix of Expectation

person's payment for execution before his teaching contract was met, and I decided to flag it and ask him about it.

Consequently, my diligence was met with passive-aggressive behavior and retribution. My otherwise spotless track record was soiled with a less-than-favorable performance review and no prospect for an annual pay increase.

This, in turn, hurt my working environment and self-esteem. I felt isolated and trapped. My boss was a trusted figurehead, and I saw no point in complaining because I believed there would be improvement in my situation.

After a few months of taking my stress home and losing sleep, I redirected my attention to activities that gave me joy outside of work. I went to the gym more and participated in a volunteer leadership program that I had Human Resources sign off on. I met a group of colleagues from that program who were very supportive and encouraged me to report my boss. They introduced me to a network of people who would later be key to getting the essential references I needed to land the job I got later, with a better boss who respects me and supports my professional endeavors.

I reported my boss, and he moved on to another position. To my knowledge, I don't believe my reporting him directly led to his departure. I think he just left to work full-time at his law practice. I have no evidence that I was the cause of his departure. I know that unplugging from my perception of his control over me freed me emotionally to alleviate my work anxiety. I decided that he would not diminish my light or joy. I had to let go of my toxic resentment towards him and release my regret over questioning him about that check.

I did nothing wrong. While there were financial consequences, I honored my values by doing my job and not abandoning my sense of integrity and honesty. It wasn't important for him to recognize that there is more to me than the administrative assistant he saw. It was important for me and my soul to acknowledge it.

His replacement was a lovely female attorney who was smart, funny, and helped make my day-to-day work environment more joyful and fulfilling.

The eternal "You" oversees your worldly roles (i.e., parent, child, partner, spouse, student, teacher, boss, employee, caregiver, etc.).

It's important to note here that I use the terms "You", "spirit you", and "Higher Self" interchangeably to describe the "authentic self".

The Sovereign Self: Unplugging from the Matrix of Expectation

I have found that a strong starting point for aligning with that Higher Self is to find a private and quiet moment to ask yourself the following:

- "What are my core values?"
- "Are they my values or values imposed upon me by others in my community?"
- "Which core values serve my highest purpose?/Which of these have I outgrown?"

Should you take on this work, discernment is critical here. Critically analyzing your core values means reviewing and modifying your belief system, a process often charged with emotion and sentimentality that you may find jarring.

In my experience, sentimentality alone is NOT a valid reason to hang on to beliefs that no longer serve you.

When I experienced regret over being vocal about the discrepancy I encountered at that job, I had to weigh the prospect of whether being honest in that situation was still a fit for me, since I experienced retribution for my action. Would that still be a core value, or was I hanging onto it for sentimental reasons? Ultimately, that decision led to my growth and felt empowering, so I knew I was honoring my Higher Self.

Your core values are not just a list of dormant ideologies. They are personal moral standards you choose to activate and live by to the best of your ability. When you falter or forget, you can always review them and check your behavior against them to objectively assess if/how you are living up to them, and modify them accordingly as you grow.

We've all seen various examples of people, political leaders, or spiritual gurus who are good at talking about their values. However, their actions can be contrary to those values.

That is your evidence that an inner conflict exists. That evidence is detectable to anyone who is paying attention to it. It's a shared human experience.

The Sovereign Self: Unplugging from the Matrix of Expectation

For me, it's not about what you say your values are; it's how you live them. Belief systems need not be verbalized. They're evident in how you honor your authentic self and treat others.

Your values should resonate with you at a gut level. Why? If your values truly honor your authentic self, they should feel like remembering who you essentially are. It should not feel like you're going against what resonates with you. It should settle you, not undo you.

Identity is not a fixed entity but a fluid construct shaped by our cultural experiences and choices. Think about the various roles we play—be it as a friend, sibling, or professional. Each role is a thread in the intricate tapestry of our lives, but they do not define the entirety of who we are.

By questioning the origins of these identities, we can untangle the truths from the illusions. Who are you when you strip away the titles?

Reflection Prompt: List the roles you inhabit. Which ones resonate most with your authentic self? Which feels inherited?

The Sovereign Self: Unplugging from the Matrix of Expectation

4. Honoring the Shadow

I was working for an older man this time. He was another under-qualified attorney who lacked experience with workplace technology and leadership qualities. At the time, I lacked the confidence to seek a better position with a salary commensurate with my experience. I believed that if I kept working hard and stayed silent, "something" would get better.

This was the same institution I worked for with the previous toxic boss who left of his own accord.

That lovely female attorney who replaced him left to raise her family. To my chagrin, this older man replaced her. Our Human Resources department was also continuously making lame excuses for why it would not issue merit raises. This newer boss was less engaged and technically savvy than any previous bosses, and my colleague was more vocal with her complaints than I was.

One day, we were meeting with a consultant for a software training session where my boss took a call and made a less-than-believable excuse to go home for the rest of the day, leaving it to me and my colleague to facilitate this meeting and fill him in later. This was just one of those "all hands on deck" situations where my coworker and I had to do all the heavy lifting and perform tasks beyond our pay grades without recompense.

I thought, "Here I go again, with a diabolical mess to carry," where I felt like a victim with no way out. At that point, I experienced a surge of anger that I felt was detectable in my appearance, so I also

The Sovereign Self: Unplugging from the Matrix of Expectation

excused myself and quietly told my coworker I needed a breather. I went out to the parking lot and sat in my car to be with my emotions.

I was overwhelmed with a sense of anger, frustration, dissatisfaction, and loss. I felt trapped and eager to leave, as with my previous boss. I was convinced I could not do better for myself because I was in this sorry predicament again, and I just cried in my car.

To say that I was feeling hopeless and powerless is an understatement. I thought I was too old (mid-40s), my marriage was failing (I knew this subconsciously, but I hadn't the courage to face that yet), and I could never find work that would properly compensate me for my twenty-plus years of experience.

There were numerous shadows that I once believed I could not face. In the philosophical and psychological world, "facing shadows" refers to confronting repressed or hidden aspects of oneself, which are called shadows.

It's a concept developed by psychotherapist Carl Jung. There is tons of information about it, and shadow work you can investigate further if you wish to do a deep dive.

I neither endorse nor discourage the reader from exploring this topic, as it is not for the faint of heart, but if this book finds you and resonates with you, consider it a viable pathway to taking stock of your belief systems. You may even consider working with a licensed therapist in your journey.

This latest work crisis taught me that my physical body and soul were rejecting my complacency for settling for the mundane for myself. I had been in this situation before. Why was I here again? I felt knots in my stomach, and my thoughts were all foggy. This response was a clear indication that I was misaligned again.

My dissatisfaction with my situation stemmed from negative self-judgment, or thought streams reinforcing that I was never worthy of a well-paid position despite my advanced degree.

It was my inner critic, a common part in the IFS framework, that engages in negative self-talk and harsh self-criticism, essentially intending to protect me from perceived threats or potential harm, specifically, manifesting the shadows of disappointment, fear of failure, and bruised ego from potential job rejection, or not being hirable anywhere else.

I also had an unhealthy attitude toward money and wealth. I was steeped in poverty consciousness. I viewed wealth as a bad thing, or the root of all evil, based on my upbringing and my parents' attitudes about wealth. Though not my own, I absorbed my parents' belief that wealth "didn't come easy for people like us." The "us" they would reference is the working class, barely "making it."

This showed up for me as my inner critic again, and a legacy burden I inherited, which led me to self-parent. I had to be the unconditional, compassionate nurturer to my inner child. I needed to tell myself that under any circumstances, I will ensure that I make it through this challenge.

The shadow manifestations I had to confront here were my impostor syndrome (a deeply held belief that I was not worthy of wealth), guilt or shame about desiring wealth, and hesitation disguised as self-protection (perpetually sabotaging my opportunities to grow). Previous opportunities with the network of people I met at my leadership program existed, but I had not yet pursued them.

These thought patterns were deeply embedded in my subconscious and lexicon. They were the toxic undercurrent of any promising opportunity that presented to me, convincing me to dismiss them as folly. Those opportunities quickly disappeared when I talked or rationalized myself out of them, leaving me with feelings of defeat and hopelessness.

Like shadows, I only noticed these agents of sabotage when I chose to shine a light on them, bringing them to my awareness and showing how they shaped my limiting beliefs.

My journey eventually led me to a better work environment. I recognized that my evolution and processes for mitigating my inner conflicts require great courage and an undying trust in myself. I had to hold myself accountable for how I received those shadows to shape my experiences.

The Sovereign Self: Unplugging from the Matrix of Expectation

When I need to self-parent, I can give myself affirmations mentally or out loud while I'm driving alone in my car. I can look over at the passenger seat and envision the child version of myself looking up at the adult me driving, seeking comfort. I would tell the child version of me that I am here for support, and ask what I can do to make the situation feel better. That brings me immediate security and comfort. It's like I'm tapping into an unlimited resource of unconditional love channeling through my body.

Shadows can emerge at any point, whether or not we have the words for them. However it happens, it's important to honor those shadows. While they can be anything but comfortable to face, you can honor them by acknowledging them as helpful growth agents. Whether or not you recognize them as shadows, they can come up in your psyche at any time, bringing up simple or complex issues you may be storing unwittingly.

My intuition compelled me to pay attention to how my body reacted to those challenges. When I would silently talk myself out of panic and overreaction in the privacy of my car, I didn't know it was a form of self-parenting until my inner compass gradually led me to dive deeper and find synchronicities, publications, and therapists that helped me fill those knowledge gaps.

Your Higher Self doesn't judge how you get to where you honor your sovereignty; it just compels you to get there.

Unpacking shadows is instrumental in getting you to acknowledge trends in your thinking patterns that can lead to actions that reflect your fear of the unknown. Fear wears many masks and can manifest in many forms. It's cyclical and can be debilitating. It can also be embarrassing and deliver huge blows to your ego, as I have learned the hard way. At the same time, I have also learned to withhold judgment of myself and to treat myself with compassion, which creates a safe space for me to grow.

Why is it important to unpack your shadows? I can tell you why it is relevant for me. I value the sovereignty of my soul. I've realized that when I ignore any shadows that come up for me, they do not subside until I recognize them and meditate on how I've carried them and fueled my fears. They will continue to come up for me in my waking state and my dreams until I deal with them. While there are times when, admittedly, ignoring my shadows can be comforting, I'll come around to asking myself if I'm growing.

I can achieve that with a brief meditation in a quiet space, setting the intention, or asking, "What do I have to learn from this particular challenge?"

I have learned (and am still learning) that facing my shadows feeds my soul. It keeps me actively questioning the status quo, however threatening it may seem to my ego or external systems.

Change and evolution don't promise to be without turbulence or trauma. However, honoring or respecting my shadows instead of the victimhood it can cause, strengthens my capacity to withstand inner turbulence and thrive alongside a constantly shifting world consciousness.

If it all sounds "new age" to you, thus giving you pause, consider the possibility of shadows that come up for you, the reader, and how you wish to face them, or not. This is not an assault on your character, but an opportunity to do your self-parenting and fearlessly embolden yourself to step outside of your comfort zone and social norms, possibly holding you back, so you can act from your truth. It's an introspection tool that requires only you to approve it.

Richard Schwartz, Ph.D., is the creator of Internal Family Systems (IFS), the therapeutic model referred to as "parts work".

Developed in the 1980s, it views the mind as an internal family made up of multiple sub-personalities, where each "part" functions similarly to a family member with specific roles and intentions, i.e., "wise part", "inner critic", "child part", etc.

He delves into therapy where he has patients call attention to those parts and channel their roles or intentions, giving voice to what those parts are attempting to call attention to.

These parts manage daily life and gate-keep our shadows.

It's a topic worth exploring for diving deeper into the shadows.

The Sovereign Self: Unplugging from the Matrix of Expectation

To truly embrace our wholeness, we must honor the shadow—the parts of ourselves we often wish to ignore. Fear, anger, and sadness can guide us, not just hinder us, directing us toward deeper understanding.

This chapter dives into the importance of shadow work, encouraging you to confront these aspects of yourself with compassion.

Reflection Prompt: Recall a recent moment of discomfort or conflict. What emotions arose? How can you use this experience to foster growth?

5. Your Inner Compass

If the reader finds themselves engaged with this material up to this point, then I propose they have some awareness that they are connected to a source beyond their three-dimensional body. You are an expression of that source, your Higher Self. As such, you are perpetually guided. You are never without it, and whether or not you choose to take ownership of this innate decision-making tool, we'll call it your *inner compass*.

Everyone has an inner compass—our innate decision-making tool tied to our core beliefs—whether or not we choose to use it.

Some can tap into it, but ignore it if they feel it doesn't align with their desired outcome.

Some fear that it unveils certain truths they aren't prepared to face. *That was my particular challenge when I chose to ignore some obvious questions and inner guidance about my failing marriage. We had grown apart, but I didn't want to admit that to myself, because it would mean I had failed at another relationship. When I finally faced it, it led to the inevitable, but we ended it amicably.*

Some may choose to weaponize it if they're operating from fear, rather than love, which is aligned with your Higher Self.

Some may transfer ownership of it to a patriarch, matriarch, or institution operating within their culture, whereby it becomes easier to shift responsibility for perceived failures.

The Sovereign Self: Unplugging from the Matrix of Expectation

In one form or another, the term "follow your heart" has been used in human discourse throughout various cultural expressions, like literature and film to emphasize the importance in taking ownership of decisions guided by one's natural ability to pursue and act on their inner compass as a means of fulfilling their destiny, doing what's right, following their bliss, taking charge of their life, finding their true love, their path to happiness.

These cultural expressions point to a collective consciousness that naturally points you back on your path. It suggests the heart's direct connection to your inner compass, which will lead you home to your authentic self.

Often, we are met with these encounters when we have reached an impasse or inner conflict that counters our intuition. We know this because "something doesn't feel right." Then our logical brain, with its recollection of fear-based reasoning, rationalizes why following your heart is foolish or childish. "What if it fails?" "That's never been done before." "That's how it's always worked in the past." "That's how I was raised," (my familiar champion of defeatist language).

The brain is guided by the heart, which sends more signals to the brain than it receives, which influences brain function [*HeartMath Institute. (2024, February 6). The Little Brain in the Heart - HeartMath Institute. https://www.heartmath.org/articles-of-the-heart/little-brain-in-the-heart/*]. Positive emotions like gratitude, love, and compassion foster coherence between the heart and brain, creating a harmonious balance.

What if we normalized the following through our collective filtration channels?:

· "Is this truly honoring my authentic self, or am I fulfilling a cultural expectation?"

· "Is this coming from self-protection or self-trust?" Each choice contracts you or expands you towards your truth.

· "How does this feel like I'm going with or against my natural progression?"

When you sit with yourself, filter all the internal chatter, and prepare to listen for answers, you will get them.

The Sovereign Self: Unplugging from the Matrix of Expectation

Like any underutilized muscle in the human body, the more you exercise it, the easier it becomes to follow inner compass guidance.

When I sat in a private space to reflect on my marriage, it was clear that we were both uncomfortable with our marital roles. My heart pushed me to find solace and comfort in the truth about our situation.

I encountered some antiquated values about marriage that I modeled from my parents, including co-dependency. It worked for them, but it was not a fit for me. We talked through them and realized we were better as good friends, minus the resentment.

You may want to try the following technique:

- Find a quiet and private space (set aside 5-10 minutes) to sit. You may lie down, but try not to fall asleep.
- Focus on the question you seek guidance for, not the expected answer.
- Close your eyes or focus on a candle's flame (in a fire-safe setting).
  - For some, focusing on one repetitive action helps quiet the mind, like tapping the index finger on the knee, floor, or on whatever furniture they're occupying.
- Set your intention on quieting your mind and all mental chatter.
- Resist the temptation to narrate your moment.
- Allow thoughts or images to come to you, not from you.

Set aside time on your calendar to do this regularly (daily or weekly), ideally, the first thing in the morning or the last thing before bed.

The Sovereign Self: Unplugging from the Matrix of Expectation

Trust your guidance. We tend to discount events or outcomes that do not happen exactly as we expected. That's usually because we are conditioned to imagine desired outcomes in ways that are comfortable to us.

We can easily set ourselves up for disappointment when the results don't transpire exactly as we envision them.

One of my earliest careers was in broadcast news. When I initially applied to this news agency in New York City (circa 1995), I wanted to be a translator. I figured it would be a way to travel and utilize my native language. I finally landed the interview and thought I surely would land the job.

Alas, the producer informed me that they were no longer hiring translators but needed a Production Assistant to start on the overnight foreign news desk. I was discouraged, but agreed. I had a feeling that this was not a dead job.

I ended up working there for about five years. I got off the overnight shift after a year helping out the news writers, writing my small editorial pieces (it taught me a lot about writing under deadlines), field producing, covering holiday parades, and coordinating live shots for breaking news events.

I never imagined the overnight desk job would yield the numerous professional experiences I accrued, fresh out of college.

We tend not to make room for the endless other opportunities that may transpire in ways that we could never have imagined—a sure way to set limitations for ourselves.

This is not a new-age concept. Neville Goddard is a 20th-century writer and lecturer who discusses this philosophy in depth. If you wish to explore this concept further, his works are helpful resources.

Contemporary societies are likely to de-prioritize the value of inner compasses, forsaking them for empirical evidence-based rationale for decision-making. While logic has its place, your inner compass should hold a place alongside logic--it has been accessible for as long as humans have existed. Its efficiency can be credited for the advances and sustainability of humankind.

The Sovereign Self: Unplugging from the Matrix of Expectation

If we can take a cue from how various species from the animal kingdom use their instinct, we are naturally equipped to navigate our world and peacefully coexist with our planet.

Your intuition is a powerful guide, often drowned out by the noise of external opinions. This chapter emphasizes the significance of trusting your inner compass. When faced with decisions, pause and listen. What does your gut tell you?

When faced with uncertainty, remember that your inner voice is a component of your true self. Cultivate this relationship through mindfulness and self-reflection.

Reflection Prompt: What inner voice did you hear in recent decision-making? Did you listen to it? If not, what held you back?

PART 3 - LIVING AS THE INFINITE SELF

6. The Practice of Presence

In the age of the cell phone and social media, it can be challenging to focus on the here and now. In a world of constant digital saturation and daily demands, it's easy to lose the present moment.

Even as we fall asleep and wake up, our brains are firing off hundreds of thoughts a minute. Have you ever rushed through a meal, mind already on unfinished work, all the other items you think are more important than nourishing your body? I'm guilty of doing that one.

If you take a moment to observe your thoughts, you'll notice how much time you spend unengaged in your present activity and how much time you spend processing thoughts about something other than the present.

I was sitting at a pristine beach in Isla Mujeres, Mexico, with a good friend. I recall her talking about our options for dinner, and her voice started fading, and my mind wandered over to thinking about the logistics of what I needed to do to prepare for my return trip. I began to feel anxious and disconnected.

"I should locate my car transport confirmation for my ride to the Cancun airport." "When do I need to complete my online check-in?"

Then I spotted a cute dog treading the beach sand, wagging its tail excitedly, which brought me back to the warm, comforting feeling of presence. I observed its thorough appreciation for the sand, the ocean, and the people around it, as it took in all the interesting sounds and smells of the tropical beach.

The Sovereign Self: Unplugging from the Matrix of Expectation

Then it dawned on me that I was squandering precious moments of my vacation. I then thought, "This is insane. I'm on vacation, with great company, and I don't have to return for two days. What a way to squander these beautiful moments I'm privileged to experience."

I was wasting time meant for my relaxation, plotting out the logistics of my return travel itinerary. How sad is that?

I laughed it off and directed my attention back to the incredible time I was there to enjoy.

What was particularly funny about that moment was that I recognized the majestic beach dog was there to bring my attention back to the present. The dog's way of being was pure presence, unburdened by cautionary calculations.

Animals do not carry the weight of juggling thoughts outside the present moment like we do.

One of the practices I now use to bring me back to the present is to think of my dog, which triggers me to stop and observe my thoughts.

When I think of my dog, I think of this sentient being that only operates from expansion. I love her unconditionally as she loves me. Thinking of her raises my frequency by activating the emotion of love, which is a direct heart connection to my soul.

Just like a human infant, she doesn't worry about how her meals get there. When she's hungry, it appears. She lives with the assumption that she's always ok. She simply IS--living entirely in the present.

It's easy to lose yourself in a frenzy of mental chatter that takes you away from the present. I find that when I'm on the go (not in my preferred quiet space), caught up in my web of mental intrigue, having nothing to do with the present, I'll:

- Take a mental pause, pay attention to my breath for centering

- Visualize my dog if I need to.

The Sovereign Self: Unplugging from the Matrix of Expectation

- Then I acknowledge all the other incidental thoughts that take me away from the here and now.

- I bring my attention back to the present.

Note that this is a quick way to bring yourself back to presence. You can do it when you're traveling, at work, etc., anytime you are not in the privacy of your own home, which differs from the practice in the previous chapter.

Taking walks, particularly through a cemetery, also helps keep me present. While it may not be everyone's cup of tea, it works wonders for me. The quiet and stillness I experience at cemeteries is like no other. It's a space where those who once lived in my world are at rest and surrounded by nature, while their spirits return to the Source. It's a stark reminder of impermanence and what humanity has in common. I pay attention to my breath and take in all my sensory encounters.

You can also find your unique triggers that bring you back to presence. Whatever resonates with you is valid.

Why does staying present matter?

Practicing presence not only grounds you mentally, but it presents an opportunity to stay connected to Source, the essential You, that is everything.

It's an opportunity to filter out the noise of anything outside of that, to engage with the moment you are experiencing. In doing so, you become acutely aware of the value of what you're experiencing. Presence allows you to step into the observer role, raising both your clarity and frequency, so you may appreciate the nuances of the mundane. It's like adjusting the focus on a camera lens or a film projector. It may call your attention to the beauty of a subtle breeze through the blade of grass in the park, or the presence of mind that is instrumental for true engagement with others.

The Sovereign Self: Unplugging from the Matrix of Expectation

Mindfulness is not a trend; it's a practice that anchors us to the present moment. This chapter explored techniques to cultivate presence in our daily lives by focusing on the here and now. We can break free from the shackles of regret and worry.

Exercise: Try a simple mindfulness exercise. Spend five minutes observing your breath. Notice the sensations, thoughts, and feelings that arise without judgment.

7. Purpose As Frequency

Earlier, I mentioned raising your frequency. Frequency is vibration; like tuning forks that resonate with musical instruments, we resonate with the universe's states of consciousness.

Resonating at lower frequencies induces negative states of consciousness that are low vibrational (i.e., insecurity, helplessness, anger, self-pity, fear). When we aim to raise our frequency, we ideally strive to enhance our mental and emotional well-being.

Engaging in higher vibrational (i.e., joy, peace, gratitude, love) practices, like mindful awareness of our thoughts, steering them away from fear-based mindsets, will advance our frequency towards the positive.

Instinctively, we can generally feel which ones are positive vs. negative.

It positions us for an existence of mental stamina and self-sufficiency, which is not easily foiled by external influences that may oppose our intuition.

I had been worrying about not having enough money. My dog was scheduled to receive a very costly surgery to repair her injured knee, which was a cost I believed would set me back for the month, even though I shared it with my ex-spouse. When I realized that I was gradually working myself up into a frenzy unnecessarily, I decided to pause and take note of my pattern. I brought my attention to my thoughts because of what I was feeling emotionally.

The Sovereign Self: Unplugging from the Matrix of Expectation

I felt helpless because I was relinquishing my perceived control of her care entirely to her surgeon. I felt insecure because I feared somehow I/we wouldn't have enough money to pay. I felt anger and a sense of failure because, somehow, I blamed myself for not having enough money to cover her procedure. I took on the persona of scarcity, and it felt awful.

Then I decided I was tired of feeling this way whenever unexpected expenses arise. This can happen to anyone. I was meant to adopt suffering as my status quo. I decided that whatever happens, she will get the care she needs, and the cost would not break me. I was so enveloped in self-pity that I completely forgot that we have pet insurance, which will reimburse most of my out-of-pocket costs.

The thought hit me through logical deduction once I decided to cancel my self-pity. When fear gets hold of you, you tend to omit certain practical truths, like the universe works with you when you act from self-trust. Once I decided that, I felt a remarkable difference, like a great sense of relief off of me, or an emotional boost.

I was grateful that the waiting for her surgery was over and that she would no longer be limping. My focus was now on the other side of this event, the assumption that it was all behind me, and it's all taken care of. I stayed in the present and in gratitude for having the great fortune of spending my days with her, being her caretaker, and knowing that we had a mutual understanding of how valuable our time together was.

This could be perceived as magical thinking, but my mental exercise took me to a higher frequency. It felt great. It was as if I were that newborn infant who had no concept of the material worries of a parent who works to provide it with food and shelter. I just knew that it would all be fine.

Sure enough, it was. Her surgery was successful, and the cost was met.

And bonus: We were at the counter and I was on my cell phone moving money around in my bank accounts to pay for her overnight boarding, when the receptionist notified us that a random woman decided to pay that cost for her—a random act of kindness. We saw the woman putting her credit card away, trying to be inconspicuous, but we thanked her anyway. She nodded, but didn't speak.

I recognized the fear and chose gratitude in that moment.

The Sovereign Self: Unplugging from the Matrix of Expectation

Purpose is not a destination but a frequency with which we resonate. This chapter invites you to explore what ignites your passion. When you align your actions with your purpose, you elevate not only your life but the lives of those around you.

Reflection Prompt: What activities make you lose track of time? How can you incorporate more of these into your daily life?

8. Global Soul, Local Heart

Our world, as we've known it historically, is changing. Global patterns are being challenged or have eroded. Namely:

The geopolitical landscape:

- The international order established after World War II, defined by an American hegemony, is in decline.

- The end of Western dominance in defining international norms is surfacing.

- Geopolitical tensions continue to increase from cyberattacks and financial market volatility.

- Escalating regional conflicts are impacting global markets and supply chains.

Social and cultural shifts:

- Globalization, digital transformation, and cyber-cultures are reshaping identity and community.

The Sovereign Self: Unplugging from the Matrix of Expectation

- Concerns about cultural homogenization and the marginalization of local traditions are fueled by cultural hybridization aided by technology and globalization.

- The inequity of access to technology globally is causing the digital divide.

- The ethical implications of artificial intelligence and data privacy continue to be debated.

Inflation pressures may rise as the world transitions to a low-carbon existence to address climate change, natural disasters, pandemics, etc.

These are a few of the global concerns that permeate our world. Those impacted will undoubtedly feel displacement, resistance, and the uncertainty that comes with change.

I am most concerned with how fear has historically held audiences captive across cultures.

For example, organized religions may use religious doctrine to convince congregants that non-believers are somehow doomed to a life less worthy than their followers.

Educational institutions may use it to discourage students from employing critical analysis to deconstruct curricular policies that may dissuade donors.

Social media algorithms capture our opinions and lock us in echo chambers, creating the illusion of widespread agreement.

When I encounter similar external patterns entering my space, for instance, viral social media posts of violent clashes between civilians and law enforcement officers that pop up on my phone screen, I try not to view them. I may catch a glimpse of it, or get a general sense of the emotional reaction it may elicit from me because it begins to stir up feelings of anxiety, anger, or frustration. That's my cue to quickly scroll past it before getting pulled into watching or reading the comment threads. I can recognize that the content is disturbing and that it's low vibrational.

While I'm not always successful at this practice, I try to be mindful of it when exposed. I would describe myself as aware, but generally willfully indifferent to charged content. I'm

The Sovereign Self: Unplugging from the Matrix of Expectation

not immune to charged content, but I hold myself accountable for how I choose to react to uncomfortable content. The information that I choose to consume, I do so with a critical eye, i.e., Who sponsors it?, What are potential biases?, How are other sources presenting it?, Why is it appearing through my algorithm?, Why is it triggering?, Does it bring up something internally I don't want to face?, Can I learn something valuable from an opposing viewpoint?

I'm not saying I endorse not staying informed about the world, but I can consume certain current events in safer doses from a healthier perspective. Media consumption is different for everyone, depending on one's background. We can gradually train ourselves to consume social media with more discernment to begin unplugging.

Fear lies in the potential threat of breaking the cocoon of comfort we hang onto, never to be breached by the vulnerability that potentially lies in being exposed to the opposing thoughts that may tear down our safety nets.

"Hate, hunger, and pride make better levers of propaganda than do love or impartiality." –Jacques Ellul, Propaganda: The Formation of Man's Attitudes.

Sovereignty is the common enemy of said external forces, which are committed to predigesting our information and feeding us variations that can be monetized or politicized. A sovereign body that pledges fealty to itself and can serve no other.

We all embody this autonomy that tethers us to a universal consciousness. It is our birthright whether or not we choose to accept it. If you are sensitive enough to recognize oppressive forces, know you are innately equipped to counter them in yourself and others.

"I freed a thousand slaves, I could have freed a thousand more if only they knew they were slaves." – Harriet Tubman.

"The soul within me no man can degrade." –Frederick Douglass.

As freedom fighters, Tubman and Douglass spoke to the crucial aspect of inner freedom, recognizing one's bondage and agency, and the resilience it takes to maintain dignity and self-worth, even when faced with brutal oppression.

The Sovereign Self: Unplugging from the Matrix of Expectation

External cultural influences can significantly undermine an individual's self-worth and autonomy in complex ways. Individuals from marginalized groups may internalize the negative stereotypes and biases prevalent in their culture, leading to feelings of inadequacy or inferiority. This can be particularly true if their experiences are constantly portrayed as "other" or "deviant" within dominant cultural narratives.

An example of that is how certain cultures frame the existence of transgender individuals as divisive and perverse. This narrative can lead to targeted harassment and abuse, much like the cases we've seen with transgender children participating in sports or using public restrooms. Some cases spiral into depression or suicide.

Such propaganda can effectively normalize a cultural consensus that certain "others" have no place in mainstream society. They were relegated to living on the fringes of society with very low self-esteem and little institutional support.

I once had a partner who practiced yoga, was health-conscious, spiritual, and seemingly attentive to me. The attention I was getting never evolved beyond the superficial. I shared an interest in their yogic journey and dietary regime, thinking we were indeed a match.

Our shared interest gradually became unbalanced when I occasionally skipped a yoga session to do my own thing, to be with my friends. When I did my own thing, it was met with passive-aggressive comments masked as light-hearted jokes on the surface, but could also be construed as light jabs at my lack of dedication. The behaviors became increasingly judgmental and hurtful.

I didn't think much of it at first because my self-esteem was considerably low at the time, and I made excuses for the demeaning behavior to justify my participation in the relationship. I was afraid of jeopardizing what I had and told myself they had my best interests at heart.

It took some time for me to piece together that efforts to rein me in were a form of control to offset my partner's insecurity. My complacency led to a mild depression and a misdirected anger that I could not articulate.

I eventually discovered their infidelity. Of course, that fast-tracked my dumping them, and I sent them packing. Had I not unmasked the infidelity, who knows how much longer I would have tolerated the

The Sovereign Self: Unplugging from the Matrix of Expectation

controlling behavior, or ignored my gut feeling of dissatisfaction that my Higher Self was signaling to me somatically.

My body responded physically as I dimmed my light to stand in their shadow. I was underweight and looked sickly. I instinctively felt that I wasn't respected, but talked myself into an unacceptable compromise. I bought into the myth that I wasn't enough. I've always had this essential navigational support that everyone has, but I chose to ignore it until I could no longer.

I use this account as a testimonial for those who choose to make themselves smaller for the sake of others or do not want to make waves by calling attention to themselves. In which case, I pose the question, "Do you believe you are worthy?"

It took me a while to gradually learn to "undim" my light, which tended to happen when I was in the company of those I admired. It was ok when others had something (talent, discipline) that I did not possess. There is no need for me to catch up. I have my unique place in the universe with my unique contributions to the greater good, as does everyone else. There is no hierarchy in the universal consciousness. Holding a space for each other to shine without judgment or competition is mutually beneficial. We all belong.

Worthiness is a fundamental universal truth that applies to all humans. Many of us can get so entrenched in identity politics that we limit ourselves to the façade of our lived experiences, when our existence goes beyond that. We are susceptible to ego-driven trappings of superficiality that incorporate materialism, envy, greed, and piety (to name a few), that keep us tethered to performative societal norms.

We are also souls (or spirits if you choose) observing an earthly experience for a limited time. If we, as a collective consciousness, operate in our daily lives from that assumption, how might that impact our world and lived experiences?

I imagine a world where humanity is on the other side of said trappings and can readily tap into their Higher Self as a constant resource for redirecting them when they veer off their path. It's a world where we no longer accept socio-economic infrastructures that oppose our spiritual autonomy.

The Sovereign Self: Unplugging from the Matrix of Expectation

We no longer defer to external figureheads defining our identities for us. We are beings who have sharpened our intuition and connection to our planet. We are our sources for inspiration. It's miraculous and transformative, truly seeing your unfiltered Self.

One of my spiritual mentors (who chooses to be anonymous) embodies that truth and has helped me to face those parts of myself that were not so pleasant to observe. He helped me to see myself, my shadows, and all. He'd say things like, "It only takes one good eye to see yourself" (he has one eye), and "Isness is your business," calling attention to how staying present and assuming the identity of your best self in the here and now is the quickest way to manifest your desires.

Societies drawing from their inner revelations and reflections about their soul journeys to inspire and encourage each other can dismantle old systems, giving way to the new.

It equips humanity with the wherewithal to contextualize challenges as observers, to piece together whatever they need to learn about themselves and their community to evolve.

While we are individuals, we are also part of a greater whole. This chapter emphasizes the balance between the local community and global consciousness. As we work towards personal growth, let us consider our impact on the world.

Reflection Prompt: Identify a cause that resonates with you. How can you take small steps to contribute locally while being mindful of the global perspective?

The Sovereign Self: Unplugging from the Matrix of Expectation

PART 4 - THE COLLECTIVE AWAKENING

9. Dismantling the Old, Seeding the New

The world is shedding its skin. Structures once seen as immovable are now cracking—exposing the hollow beneath the hustle, the illusion beneath the order. Globally, the collapse of economic systems, the erosion of trust in institutions, and the rising cry for planetary and personal healing are not signs of failure. They are signs of awakening.

We are not simply watching systems break down—we are being invited to reimagine what's possible beyond them.

From a spiritual lens, this is the necessary death before the rebirth. What no longer resonates is dissolving. Not to punish us, but to prepare us. The invitation is not to fear the unraveling, but to meet it with presence, discernment, and grace.

A Personal Unraveling

There was a time when I believed that following the rules was the path to peace. I measured success through compliance, stability, and performance. I wore armor on top of my adaptability, pleasing and producing in the name of acceptance.

But slowly, something began to ache.

The Sovereign Self: Unplugging from the Matrix of Expectation

There wasn't a single moment of collapse, just a steady erosion of energy. My spirit would tighten at places that once felt safe. My body would resist what my mind tried to normalize.

I once had a circle of friends with whom I shared many spiritual bonds. We met semi-regularly to do spiritual work, meditations, have deep metaphysical conversations, and occasionally meet socially. We comforted each other through hardships and challenges, offering support if possible.

One day, we were all hanging out having coffee, when the teenage daughter of one of the male members made an unusual comment alluding to the fact that their father had an inappropriate relationship with them. We'll leave it at that to protect the privacy of those involved.

A few of us and I heard what she said. There was a brief moment of silence. The child's father was not in the room at the time. He was a respected member of our group. A few of us discussed it for a few days with some disbelief and group doubt about what we heard and what we thought we heard.

For some time, I wrestled with what I thought I heard, but knew instinctively that this was the beginning of the end of our group. My body tensed up around these people; our conversations were now tainted and seemed hypocritical. The resistance was palpable. My inner compass told me that I had gotten all I could from this group and that they had some things to work out. I knew there would be a ripple effect.

Eventually, there was a lot of infighting, our collective energy eroded, miscommunications, and betrayal. It all came to a head at one of our gatherings, where it all came out (not by me). That person glossed over the statement as if they had never heard it.

While it was painful for me to face, it was no surprise, because my spirit amplified this situation for me early on, and I knew there was no opportunity for me to grow. I was grateful for this experience, but it came to an end. I left.

Eventually, the choice became clear: either continue fragmenting myself to maintain the illusion, or risk everything to become whole and honor myself.

Leaving that structure—internally and externally—felt like free-falling. I thought I was without a support system (we are never without one). I felt a sense of loss. In the stillness that followed, I remembered myself. Not as a role. Not as a label, but as a presence. A frequency. A being. Ensuring I keep my frequency high is a justifiable reason to break away from a collective that opposes it.

The breakdown became a breakthrough.

Grounded Practices for Soul-Led Rebuilding

When things fall apart—within us or around us—it's natural to seek quick fixes. But soul-led rebuilding doesn't rush.

Here are practices I return to:

1. Breathe Before You Bind

In moments of confusion, pause before committing to the old. Let breath become your compass. Let stillness speak first.

When I sense I've outgrown something I'm no longer passionate about, I breathe and listen for direction.

2. Notice Without Judgment

What beliefs arise under stress? What behaviors do you default to? Awareness is not condemnation—it's an invitation. Don't shame the old. Witness it. Thank it. Release it.

When I make bad decisions, I tend to default to feeling angry and regretful, which wastes a lot of energy, and judgmental. I am learning to observe these situations as a learner. Sometimes I pretend I'm an extraterrestrial, grateful for the opportunity to observe how I experience life. I embody this persona, so it's easier for me to detach emotionally and then release it, once I've reviewed what I can learn from it.

3. Discernment Over Reaction

Not every invitation is meant to be accepted, especially in times of change. Let alignment—not urgency—guide you.

I found myself imposing a timeline on myself for the publication of this book because it had been lying dormant for so long. Suddenly, I felt rushed once I had an outline of my chapters, because I had finally picked this up again, both self-imposed and from potential copy editors, to send drafts. I felt anxious and vulnerable at this prospect. I soon realized the publication of this book would happen exactly when it was

The Sovereign Self: Unplugging from the Matrix of Expectation

supposed to happen. No sooner. No later. When it feels right, I'll publish. This isn't my old broadcasting job. What deadline?

4. Remember You Are Not Alone

Transformation is personal, but not solitary. Connect with others who are also unlearning, softening, and returning. Sacred community strengthens the soil. Most importantly, you always have yourself.

5. Seeding New Agreements

When we release what no longer serves us, we make space for what does.

But rather than reaching for ready-made replacements, what if we slow down and listen for what wants to emerge?

When we choose to work at dismantling dated narratives, it can be accompanied by growing pains that take us by storm. This discomfort can be met with self-compassion to help alleviate that emotional distress.

I mentioned earlier how allowing myself to exist in a judgment-free zone and treating myself with compassion offers me that room to evolve. I encourage the reader to do the same for themselves.

What new agreements could we make—not from fear or habit—but from truth?

- I agree to value presence over performance.
- I agree to honor intuition as intelligence.
- I agree to speak my truth even when my voice trembles.
- I agree to soften where I once guarded.
- I agree to be a vessel for the sacred in everyday life.

These are not rules. They are roots.

The Sovereign Self: Unplugging from the Matrix of Expectation

Becoming the Soil

Transformation begins within. This chapter is not a call to force change, but to become the soil for it. It is a reminder that dismantling outdated beliefs and structures is not destruction. It is devotion to truth.

Yes, change can be uncomfortable. But that discomfort is often the first signal of awakening, the ache before the bloom.

Let your Infinite Self rise to meet the new, as the old crumbles.

Reflection Prompt: What outdated beliefs do you hold? How can you begin to challenge and transform them?

The Sovereign Self: Unplugging from the Matrix of Expectation

10. Infinite You

Milarepa was a Tibetan yogi and poet from the 11th and 12th centuries whose early life was about suffering and wrongdoing. His father died when he was young, and his uncle and aunt took over the family property. They mistreated him, his mother, and his sister. His mother wanted revenge, which led Milarepa to learn black magic. He caused the deaths of many, including his relative. He also cast spells to destroy the villagers' crops, which led to a famine.

His acts of revenge sated him at first, but then he felt deep remorse and inner torment. He realized that he was perpetuating a vicious cycle of suffering, which marked a turning point in his life. He sought a spiritual path to atone for his sins and find freedom.

He eventually became a disciple of Marpa Lotsawa, a renowned Tibetan Buddhist master. Marpa subjected Milarepa to intense trials and tests to purify his karma, thus challenging his commitment to the spiritual path. His trials included repeatedly building and dismantling towers. Through these experiences, Milarepa learned the importance of humility, detachment, perseverance, and dedication.

Milarepa then retreated to the mountain for intense meditation and self-discipline. He faced his inner demons and temptations, representing his shadows, which he would eventually overcome.

The Sovereign Self: Unplugging from the Matrix of Expectation

While shadows outwardly appear to be tormentors, they are here to help us evolve.

Milarepa's struggles included emotional turmoil, isolation, and endurance through physical hardships. He ultimately attained enlightenment through his unwavering dedication and practice, thus proving that even a murderer can become a Buddha.

His quest to repair his wrongdoings speaks to the importance of inner reflection, the integration of conflicting aspects of his pursuit of spiritual transcendence in his soul journey, self-discovery, and personal transformation.

Being present: Milarepa's transformation began by becoming mindful of the suffering he caused. Something at his core tormented him and prompted him to choose love over anger and revenge, which are consequences of fear.

Overcoming shadows: His willingness to face his past misdeeds, endure trials, and engage with his inner demons led him to enlightenment and liberation from suffering.

Milarepa's struggle with "inner demons" resonates with me the most. Particularly, when Milarepa's cave is overrun by demons. Initially, he tries to teach them the Dharma, but they make fun of him. Then he offers them his home and even his life, which causes them to vanish.

This highlights the power of acceptance and surrender in overcoming inner turmoil.

Likewise, when I questioned my self-worth during my toxic relationship with the yogi, my shadow of unworthiness manifested as self-sabotaging behavior, like allowing myself to be criticized for imperfections (skipping yoga to be with my friends). It also manifested as perfectionism and people-pleasing (dimming my light).

Recognizing these saboteurs led to the ultimate necessity of terminating the relationship and transcending those shadows.

Elevating one's frequency: His relentless pursuit of spiritual realization through meditation and devotion led to a profound shift in his awareness and inner state.

The Sovereign Self: Unplugging from the Matrix of Expectation

His trial with "repeatedly building and dismantling towers mirrors my having to dismantle the spiritual network I had built. Each tower he built and demolished can be seen as a symbol of ego and attachment. His labor, hopes of completing a tower, and the frustration at its demolition symbolized the constant attachment to worldly achievement and the ego's desire for recognition.

It also symbolized the futility of worldly pursuits. The repetitive nature of the task amplified the impermanence of all worldly endeavors and the ultimate futility of seeking lasting satisfaction in external accomplishments.

My task was to let go of my attachments to my spiritual group once I came to a profound realization about what was happening.

I was frustrated and sad when I had to let it go, but I realized it couldn't last forever, especially when I stopped evolving.

Milarepa's journey of deconstructing your values and deepening your connection to your authentic self represents a universal model for your path to the infinite you.

Each of us has a unique journey and can arrive at an understanding of our authentic self at any given time and pace, depending on what we are ready to receive. Like a guardian angel, the love and support we can harness from our Higher Self is an infinitely accessible source for wisdom, judgment-free, and compassionate.

The more I tap into it for attunement, the more hopeful I am that the state of presence it breathes into us will inform humanity for generations to come.

I envision a world where cultures, awakened to the power of being present, will no longer view wars and cultural clashes as a viable consciousness for progressive societies. Upholding the state of presence as a universal standard is beneficial not only to personal growth and its ability to enhance our lived experiences, but also infectious.

When presence is normalized, we can see evidence of it in the lexicon of everyday communication, in the expression of various art forms (cinema, music, etc.). We would see the demise of group thinking. People readily answer the instinct to speak up when their opinions oppose popular beliefs and are met with open-minded support.

The Sovereign Self: Unplugging from the Matrix of Expectation

It holds the potential to be modeled by others who are drawn to raising their frequencies to match it. It is one of the many ways that this collective consciousness can serve the greater good.

When we can stand up against cultural marginalization, bodily autonomy is no longer a revolutionary act; it is accepted as a social norm on a global scale, and we can collectively hold space for further advances in humanity.

Now ask yourself, "Who am I when I am no longer afraid?"

Fear can take on many forms, dictating our lives in ways that can be obvious or so subtle that we barely take notice. History has shown us how it corrupts our capacity to own and live up to our full potential on a global scale. When left unchecked, we subject ourselves to the enslavement of our souls. It is human nature to coexist peacefully and as free spirits. Surrendering to conditions (willfully or by force) that oppose it goes against our nature.

When contemplating this question, consider it from the framework of the spirit/soul you are. No race, class, religion, ethnicity, relationship, family, or cultural ties obligate you to anyone or anything. You are a sovereign entity weighing in on your life experience. What do you wish to experience and contribute to the greater good? What are you passionate about? Remember, there are no limits.

If you find yourself setting limitations on yourself, consider if those stem from fear-based shadows.

Consider what we discussed so far, and if any are applicable here.

Ask your Higher Self for clarity and insight. Then wait for an unfiltered response. Look around, listen, and journal what happens. Discernment is also important. For instance, distinguishing practical fear, i.e., "Go stand in front of oncoming traffic," vs. useless fear, i.e., "I'm too old to consider going back to school."

Look for synchronicities, such as when your eyes fall on the title of a book, or you hear some dialogue or sounds in or outside of your location that seem oddly timely and resonate with you. Don't judge it. It's no coincidence. That is how the universe responds to you when you are connected.

The Sovereign Self: Unplugging from the Matrix of Expectation

As you become more comfortable receiving communications, you can integrate certain rituals, like writing letters to the Infinite You, as you sharpen your intuitive tools.

Have you ever experienced a moment when you have a dream, or a fleeting thought that comes back to the forefront of your recollection when you encounter it elsewhere, like someone else says it or does it before you've expressed it out loud? Or maybe you've had a déjà vu?

I've always felt that any thought or desire that any sentient, intelligent being has dreamt up, in the waking or dream state, is created in the universal consciousness. As quickly as it's conceived, it exists somewhere in some dimension, waiting to be manifested.

There are very few original thoughts or expressions. Somehow, someone can tap into the multitude of expressions we continuously co-create with our infinite selves. This predates oral traditions, the written word, and technologies.

As such, creating something "new" is more about the unique vibration alignment we connect to. It's a personal experiential filter through which universal truths are expressed. It not only feeds our souls, but it also adds to the wealth of knowledge that upholds the integrity of Source.

The vastness of our soul's connection to consciousness is beyond comprehension and rife with mysteries; it continues to reveal itself to humanity as we continue to unplug from the Matrix and resolve to deconstruct prefabricated identities meant to divert our attention from remembering our authenticity.

We are all facets of an infinite source navigating a unique human experience. Our acquired knowledge goes back with us to the Higher Self.

Like a drop of water in a vast ocean, we are a drop of unique experiences. We are a unique piece to a vast puzzle within our place in the universe.

If you have ever doubted that your existence has any significance or meaning, take comfort in honoring the value of your presence. No other sentient being or cultural institution can deconstruct your worth without your consent.

The Sovereign Self: Unplugging from the Matrix of Expectation

As we conclude this journey, remember that you are infinite in your potential. This chapter serves as a reminder of the power within you to create, transform, and live authentically. Each step you take towards embracing your true self contributes to the collective awakening we explored earlier.

When I began this journey, I thought awakening was about learning something new, or that the truth was hidden somewhere far away, waiting for me to find it. The Sovereign Self doesn't come from the external; it pre-existed the stories and labels before the veil was pulled over my eyes.

The work was never to seek the truth elsewhere. It was to remember it within. The veil was fear, dated beliefs, expectations spun together by others, and my acceptance. Every moment I honor my inner compass, another thread comes loose until it all disappears, making me the author of my story.

I hope that the veil falls for you and that these words give you the courage to keep steadily pulling at the threads that hold together your inherited fears and belief systems that no longer serve your higher purpose, until your world is the one your Sovereign Self has chosen.

You are reading this book because the shift within you has begun.

When the veil falls for you, you will know what I now know:

- You are not your fears, failures, wounds, and masks.
- Choose presence over illusion.
- Choose your path, not the one chosen for you.
- You have always been infinite and free.
- You are the Sovereign Self.

Reflection Prompt: What does living authentically mean to you? Write a personal manifesto outlining your commitment to embracing your Sovereign Self.

The Sovereign Self: Unplugging from the Matrix of Expectation

AI DISCLOSURE STATEMENT

In the interest of transparency and integrity, AI was used as a tool for this work in the following ways:

- Historical validation and research access: Used to validate historical assertions and access qualitative research data and current events. The insights, concepts, or existing research came from the author. AI was used to ascertain specific dates, times, eras, and particular historical events, access existing academic/scholarly research. The author checked the responses and validated them through additional manual research.

- Analyzing patterns and themes: This work, in its original form, was several years of the author's journals, which included dreams, personal relationships, meditation work, shadow work, reflection of core values, and intuitive downloads. Those pages were all digitized, converted to text, added to the working untitled manuscript, and then edited and refined manually by the author. All of those entries were then manually grouped according to themes. They were edited manually to isolate the desired content for this manuscript. AI was then utilized as a secondary step to help the author analyze the drafted manuscript and develop chapter names based on the content. The analysis was then reviewed and edited by the author and incorporated only if it was aligned with the author's perspective.

- Mirroring and conversational development: AI was used conversationally to discuss the concepts and core insights that are the basis for this framework and mirror them back to the writer. AI was used for these conversations to check spelling and grammar and recite concepts to the writer. When AI "asked" clarifying questions or "requested" elaboration during these conversations, the author evaluated whether such prompts helped articulate existing thoughts more clearly. All substantive responses and developments came from the author's human reflection and analysis.

- Simplification of concepts: Some of the lofty/verbose/complex/abstract concepts were analyzed by AI, and the writer then assessed the output introspectively, as a curious human thinker. The initial concept was occasionally refined, ensuring that its essential message was intact and not compromised, and only then ratified and included.

The fundamental framework, insights, and arguments presented in this work are entirely the intellectual property and creative output of the author. AI served as a research and organizational tool, a designer (generating relevant images and book cover art), a grammatical and formatting expert (punctuation/flow/phrasing), a content reviewer, and a source validator, not as a creative collaborator or co-author.

GLOSSARY

The All that Is / Universal Consciousness: The universal consciousness, described as all-knowing and omnipresent, is the source that compelled the author's writing and is connected to all sentient beings. It is proposed that "any thought or desire that any sentient, intelligent being has dreamt up... is created in the universal consciousness" and exists somewhere waiting to be manifested.

Shapeshifting Spirits and Unseen Worlds: Shapeshifting figures in folklore, mythology, and the author's encounter that awakened their awareness of other sentient beings and "alternate realities" beyond the "waking world," where intuition and feelings lead.

The Concept of "The Matrix": As a metaphor for societal structures (government, education, media, cultural norms) that can control thoughts, beliefs, and understanding. It helps when deconstructing identity and discerning the authentic self from social constructs.

Poverty Consciousness: Delving into the ingrained attitudes toward money and wealth that may stem from upbringing and cultural absorption, often leading to self-sabotage.

Heart-Brain Coherence: The understanding that the heart sends more signals to the brain than vice versa, influencing brain function, and that positive emotions like gratitude, love, and compassion foster coherence between the heart and brain.

Socratic Method and Dialectical Reasoning: These philosophical approaches involve questioning assumptions, clarifying ideas, identifying contradictions, and analyzing arguments by challenging one view with its opposite to find truth and understanding.

Indigenous Wisdom and Decolonization of Knowledge: Understanding Indigenous epistemologies can challenge dominant Western knowledge systems, promoting a more nuanced view of the world, social justice, and a deeper connection to land and community.

Art and Creative Expression for Social Commentary: How artists use their work to reflect and critique societal norms, provoke thought, and raise awareness about issues like inequality and injustice, leveraging techniques like satire and symbolism, including through digital platforms.

Collective Mindfulness: Engaging in group meditation practices to create a shared energy field, promoting unity, compassion, empathy, and activism within a community.

Critical Pedagogy: This educational approach emphasizes learners as active participants, challenging dominant narratives, making biases visible, and fostering intellectual humility.

Critical Thinking and Open Dialogue: The importance of creating safe spaces for diverse perspectives, challenging assumptions by seeking evidence, and practicing self-awareness to address biases.

Journaling and Self-Reflection: As a safe space to explore thoughts, identify patterns, process emotions, challenge negative beliefs, and gain mental clarity, fostering a more positive and realistic perspective.

Purpose as Frequency and Raising Your Vibration: The concept of aligning with a high vibrational frequency, akin to a musical tuning fork, by engaging in positive states of consciousness (joy, peace, gratitude, love) to enhance mental and emotional well-being and elevate one's life.

Social Activism and Community Organizing: Mobilizing individuals through collective action, advocacy, building coalitions, and even silent activism (e.g., boycotts) to address systemic injustices and promote social change.

Sovereignty of the Soul and Inherent Worthiness: The understanding that individuals possess an innate worthiness and autonomy that tethers them to a universal consciousness, and the importance of valuing this sovereignty.

Synchronicities: Exploring these meaningful coincidences as a form of communication from the universe when one is connected, such as eyes falling on a book title or hearing timely dialogue.

Unplugging from Dogma: Choosing to detach from societal dogma and external affirmation to pursue passions and honor the Higher Self unapologetically.

FURTHER READING

For readers interested in delving deeper into the concepts and figures discussed in *The Sovereign Self: Unplugging from the Matrix of Expectation*, the following resources and topics are suggested for further exploration:

• **C.L.R. James's The Black Jacobins (1938):** This book provides a historical illustration of how the exploitation of enslaved labor on plantations, such as those on Hispaniola (modern-day Haiti), produced the commodities that underpinned the growth and expansion of early capitalism in Europe and the Americas.

• **Carl Jung and Shadow Work: Carl Jung's works on Analytical Psychology**: To understand the psychological concepts of the collective unconscious and the archetype of the shadow, foundational for understanding "shadow work".

• **St. John of the Cross's "The Dark Night of the Soul": Dark Night of the Soul, written ca. 1584, English translation by E. Allison Peers, 1957** (the most common translation): This spiritual text offers insight into a transformative phase of purification and introspection.

• **Neville Goddard's Works (Multiple works from 1939 to 1966, including his compilation Neville Goddard: The Collected Works, 2020)**: These writings offer resources for exploring the philosophy of trusting one's inner guidance and the power of imagination in manifestation.

• **Richard Schwartz, Ph.D., on IFS, Internal Family Systems Therapy (1994)**: To learn more about this therapeutic model, also known as "parts work," which views the mind as an internal family with various sub-personalities (e.g., "wise part," "inner critic," "child part").

- **Jacques Ellul's Propaganda: The Formation of Man's Attitudes (1962)**: This book provides insights into how certain human emotions, such as "hate, hunger, and pride," can be more effective levers for propaganda than "love or impartiality".

- **Harriet Tubman (Sarah H. Bradford's Harriet, The Moses of Her People, 1886) and Frederick Douglass (Autobiographies: My Bondage and My Freedom, 1855 and Narrative of the Life of Frederick Douglass, an American Slave, 1845)**: Their experiences and statements speak to the crucial aspect of inner freedom, recognizing one's bondage and agency, and the resilience needed to maintain dignity and self-worth even under severe oppression.

- **Milarepa's Life and Teachings W.Y. Evans-Wentz's Tibet's Great Yogi Milarepa (1928)**: The journey of this 11th and 12th-century Tibetan yogi and poet serves as a universal model for inner reflection and spiritual transcendence.

- **Frida Kahlo's Art (Hayden Herrera's Frida: A Biography of Frida Kahlo, 1983)**: A comprehensive biography that explores Kahlo's significant themes of identity, feminism, and inequity.

ABOUT THE AUTHOR

Carmid Vileramis, author of "The Sovereign Self: Unplugging from the Matrix of Expectation," guides readers on a transformative journey to discover their authentic selves. Vileramis's literary path began as a deeply personal journal, ultimately compelled by "The All that Is"—a universal consciousness.

Vileramis's profound insights are rooted in a lifetime of unique experiences.

Vileramis openly shares personal struggles, such as a midlife career crisis that exposed ingrained poverty consciousness and an unhealthy relationship with wealth.

This led to a crucial confrontation with inner "shadows" like impostor syndrome, guilt, shame, and fear of failure/success.

Similarly, a past controlling relationship highlighted the importance of self-worth and trusting inner signals. Vileramis also benefited from a spiritual mentor who guided him in confronting difficult aspects of the self and embracing presence.

These experiences fueled a profound commitment to living as a true co-creator of life, rather than passively accepting external circumstances. Vileramis champions unplugging from societal dogma and the need for external affirmation, emphasizing that an individual's worthiness is an inherent, universal truth.

In *The Sovereign Self: Unplugging from the Matrix of Expectation*, Vileramis empowers readers to deconstruct inherited identities, embrace their Higher Self, and trust their inner compass; the heart, which serves as a North Star for passion and purpose. The book advocates for the practice of presence, raising one's frequency through mindful awareness, and transforming challenges into opportunities for growth.

Vileramis envisions a world where humanity operates from this awakened consciousness, actively dismantling old, divisive systems and fostering a collective environment where self-discovery and bodily autonomy are accepted as social norms.

Vileramis's work is a testament to the transformative power of introspection, courage, and unconditional self-compassion.

The author transparently discloses the use of AI in the book's development, noting its role in historical validation, analyzing themes from personal journals, and conversational development.

However, Vileramis affirms that all fundamental insights, arguments, and creative output remain the author's intellectual property.

Carmid Vileramis invites readers to embark on their journey of self-remembrance and sovereignty, underscoring that each individual is a unique facet of an infinite source, constantly co-creating their reality.

www.ingramcontent.com/pod-product-compliance
Lightning Source LLC
Chambersburg PA
CBHW022120090426
42743CB00008B/932